A YOUNG MAN'S GUIDE to GETTING SOME

A YOUNG MAN'S GUIDE to GETTING SOME

HOW TO WIN THE GIRL OF YOUR DREAMS
with respect and class
IN THE AGE OF SEXTING AND SWIPING

MALCOLM CHENU

CONTENTS

PREFACE

You're thinking about getting some right now, aren't you? Go on, admit it. It's perfectly natural. More natural than anything, actually. Getting some is literally the meaning of life. The universe began with a Big Bang after all. If you're still not convinced, just ask the father of evolution, Charles Darwin who, by the way, fathered ten human children too, despite having a beard that was more Santa than hipster.

A few billion years ago a few horny cells, who had until then simply been splitting, began merging to share genetic material. They found it was more fun getting into each other's membranes. And so 'getting some' began. The practice caught on and now all life forms - from basic to complex - shag.

One of these basic life forms - the human male - pretty much spends his life trying to get some,

YOU'RE THE KIND OF GUY
who takes the
HIGH ROAD
in your relationships
WITH WOMEN.

SLEAZE, LIES
AND DISRESPECT
are for LESSER MEN

which is also natural. Lying to girls, trying to get them drunk or sending dick pics with winky face emoticons followed by an eggplant, isn't.

Getting some is in your blood. Every one of your ancestors got some, from your first ancestral cell all the way through to your parents. Gross? Sure. But if just one of your forebears hadn't got some, you wouldn't be here wondering how you will ever look your grandma in the eye again.

Getting some is hardwired into you but here you are not getting some. Let's fix that.

So what's the secret to getting some?

The answer is both astonishingly simple and infuriatingly complex. It's about little things and big things and sweet nothings. Showing more style and less butt crack; listening to her even when she talks during the footy; offering a foot massage without thinking it's foreplay. It's about putting her on a pedestal, even if that makes it harder to knock her off.

It's about being honest and honourable. It's about confidence. It's about being you, maybe with a few of the rough edges sanded away.

Which brings us back to evolution. Consider

the peacock. Natures' most metrosexual animal is certainly ostentatious and those feathers are hardly a good way to hide from predators. For something so edible, glam and slow-moving to have survived natural selection - not to mention the shit he must get from other animals - he must get plenty.

He's not telling lies, stuffing socks down his pants or a pouring on enough aftershave to gag a donkey. He's not texting 'Hey gorgeous, wanna Netflix n chill?' at midnight. He's just being his best self. And the peahen can see he is not afraid to be himself and he is trying to please her.

And it works. Ever seen the peacock on an endangered species list? Exactly.

DISCLAIMER

Any implication that all women are the same and will all respond to the same treatment is regretted. There are around three-and-a-half billion of them and pigeon holing them is ridiculous. However, insofar as they are to be treasured and desired for the heights to which they can take you in the form of love and its related rewards, they are the same.

TAKING THE HIGH ROAD TO GETTING SOME *is different.* THERE ARE A FEW THINGS YOU NEED TO KNOW *and do* BEFORE YOU SET OFF

SECTION ONE

SOME BASICS

PORNOGRAPHY *is not* REAL LIFE

It may surprise you to know that apparently they have pornography on the internet these days. Putting aside the risk of repetitive strain injury, the main problem with virtual sex is it's not getting you virtually anywhere. Your goal is not to become a lonely - albeit highly-skilled - masturbator. (Unless this *is* your thing, in which case you should follow your dream and be the best damn wanker you can.)

Watching a lot of porn is destructive to the soul. It is not keeping your eye on the ball. Well it is, it's just the wrong ball. Sure, porn stars won't break your heart, use your razor or hog the doona but they're NOT REAL!!

Girls, mostly, are not heavy porn consumers.

Some are of course, and if you find one who shares your passion, great! But many find it creepy and wonder why guys waste their time in the virtual world when there is a real world with actual girls in it right outside.

At its core, pornography is abuse. Especially hard-core. Women's sexuality does not exist for the gratification of men. Not many little girls dream of being a porn-star when they grow up.

What constitutes a *lot* of porn is subjective but if you open more than one porn browser at a time or are trawling BDSM chatrooms under the name HotnHornyShavedFilipinaCowgirl(bi), then you have probably crossed the line. Too much porn can lead to other delusions. Not all girls want to wear a studded leather harness and be spanked. Not all penises are huge. Not all home-delivered pizzas are paid for like that.

It may be best to avoid the subject on a date too. It's great to talk movies but admitting you saw a different version of *Eat Pray Love* or arguing that the plot from *The Notebook* was stolen from *Spring Break Ho's Go Wild IV* may not get you to dessert.

YOU'RE THE KIND
of guy
WHO KEEPS HIS
PORN
CONSUMPTION TO
A MINIMUM

GET A CHIC CHICK TO DRESS YOU

If your idea of dressing to impress involves washing your 'No Fat Chicks' tee-shirt and wearing your good thongs, it may be time for a makeover.

Go shopping with a stylish girl you trust and be prepared to spend a month's pay. Or go to a high-end boutique and tell the shop assistant to make you look hot. Restyling yourself will give you a burst of confidence that will outlast the short-term Visa pain. Pay more than $10 for a haircut.

Look through a men's fashion mag and find a look to suit you and your body shape. Admiring the cut of a pair of trousers on a male model does not make you gay. You are only gay if you want to have sex with the model. Which is fine, as long as it's cool with the model.

Don't be fanatical about your appearance. She is the beautiful one, not you. If you would rather be with yourself because you are unbelievably gorgeous or you purse your lips when you see a camera, then - as the great Bieber said – *'you can go and love yourself'*.

Guys shouldn't spend hours preening themselves. Shave (or trim), shower, clean fingernails, not too much aftershave, fashionable clothes that fit and shoes. If your beauty routine takes more than half-an-hour – or if you have ever used the words 'my beauty routine' - you may have a problem.

YOU ARE THE KIND OF GUY WHO TAKES PRIDE IN HIS APPEARANCE. *you are* NOT THE KIND OF GUY WHO CANNOT PASS A MIRROR WITHOUT HELP

YOU ARE NOT

merely a

LIFE-SUPPORT

SYSTEM

FOR YOUR

PECKER

THE PECKERING ORDER: YOUR PENIS AND YOU

First you need to establish who is in charge. Once this is decided and you have accepted that your penis is the boss, you need to make him understand you still have some rights. He must understand that 'no means no'. He does not have to deal with the guilt, regret or other consequences of his actions.

Don't fixate about your wang. If you have a dick image problem, deal with it. There's not much you can do about it anyway. Creams, pumps and other so-called enlargement aids do not work. It is what it is. There are three-and-a-half billion meat swords in the world and yours is not the biggest, smallest or prettiest. It's probably more normal than you think. And - most importantly - it's what you do with it that counts.

She doesn't care nearly as much about Mr Winky as you do.

And don't give it a nickname. Mr Winky or anything else. Especially something that could be a Marvel action hero.

SEXTING

In a word – no.

Classy guys don't sext. Flirty is fine but only arseholes put the hard word on, personally or electronically. Just when she was thinking she'd finally met a cool guy, you destroy it all with the stroke of a 'send' key. Your clumsy, romance-free tactic has killed your chances and probably upset her too. Now you are just another lazy sleazebag. And she will tell people.

Here's a quick quiz: Which of these texts do you think is more likely to succeed?

a) 'Wanna catch up?' or

b) 'Wanna lick my junk?'

Ironically, option b) will almost certainly ensure your junk remains unlicked. It's amazing how many guys go to the junkyard and are surprised by the ensuing epic fail.

NEVER send dick pics. Even if asked. You don't demonstrate you are a real man by proving you have a penis. She probably already knows this. If you want to be a real man, take her out.

And NEVER ask her for nudes. If you receive one, it is for your eyes only. If you share it with the hashtag #I'mHittingThat, you are the ultimate scumbag and will never be trusted again. Trust is a powerful aphrodisiac but it shatters easily and cannot be rebuilt.

YOU'RE THE KIND OF GUY WHO PREFERS PERSONAL CONTACT TO SLEAZY SEXTING

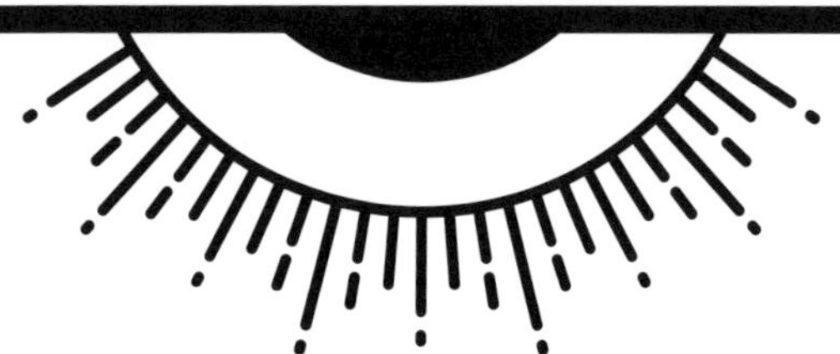

FAINT HEART NEVER WON FAIR MAIDEN

Never a truer word was spoken. Wallflowers don't get their stamens pollinated.

If you are shy by nature, getting some may seem a long way off. Fainting, sweating, throwing up in your mouth or wetting your pants are not traits she imagines in the man of her dreams.

Shyness can be hard to overcome but there are things you can do. Practice conversations in the mirror, lift your volume, learn to breathe and relax. Imagine yourself confident and assured. Say good morning to people when you get into a lift, ask your barista or waiter if they're having a good day. If your shyness is really serious, talk to a GP.

Stand up straight and speak clearly. Maintain eye

contact and smile - and not in a freaky stalker-dude way. Talk about stuff you know. Ask her questions that require more than a yes/no answer. It may not be the best opening line but after a while you can admit to her you are initially shy around women you find attractive.

Some say it is a good idea to visualise people naked if you are nervous. Whether this works for you will depend on your level of self-control.

Don't try to be super-cool or smooth if you're not. Just be genuine and have the guts to have a go. Take a risk. Maybe you'll crash and burn. Maybe not. Either way, you'll probably learn something and be better next time.

YOU'RE THE KIND OF

GUY

WHO HAS A

GO

CELEBRATE BEAUTY

In everyone and everything. Get into the habit of noticing loveliness. Everyone – especially women - has something beautiful about them. Sometimes you may have to be creative – like at the all-you-can-eat-night at the shopping mall food court - but it is important that you try.

Total honesty is not always the way to go: "Those track-pants make your love handles look really hot" and "I love the way your zits capture the moonlight" are good examples.

If you don't feel right after complimenting a girl, you haven't got the hang of it yet. Practice on something easier and less likely to slap you. Art, nature, stars and architecture all offer excellent beauty-spotting opportunities. It may be in the eye of the beholder but the man who appreciates beauty will attract beauty. The key is sincerity. And not just fake sincerity - girls can smell this a mile away.

Women are gorgeous, stunning, striking, elegant and a dozen other adjectives. And none more so than yours. Tell her she's looking good even when she is just lounging around in gym gear without make-up. And when she makes a special effort, you must reward her with more than just a grunt of relief that she is finally actually ready to go out, even though the movie has started and you need another shave.

When you spend your life appreciating beauty, the air is sweeter, the days are sunnier and even the traffic is less annoying. You'll stand taller, feel happier and enjoy a great deal more sex.

YOU'RE THE KIND OF
GUY WHO LOOKS FOR
AND CELEBRATES

BEAUTY

EVERYWHERE
& every day

THE LIST

Whether it's a basic mental checklist or a formal agenda written on a parchment with platypus blood and burned on the flame of a frangipani-scented candle with the ashes scattered in the wind at midnight during a full moon, she has a list of attributes she is looking for in a man.

Nothing on The List is unreasonable – this is her List and she has every right to it. The List may include smart, funny, good kisser, stable job, nice to friends, children and animals, not controlling, sweet smile, good bod and owns an island.

You probably have a List too but 'Has a heartbeat and a vajayjay' is not exactly narrowing the field, is it?

Deal breakers will be at the top of The List. Must be a non-smoker, love cats, minimal tatts, be able to locate a clitoris with minimal assistance etc... Whatever. Just be aware she is ticking them off one-by-one.

Do not pretend to be what you are not just to satisfy

The List. If you have a naked chick tattooed on your arse, smoke six bongs a day, kick cats for fun and think a clitoris is a Greek dessert, this is not the girl for you. Actually, you have no chance with anyone. Your hand probably rejects you.

Do not resent it if you don't fit her exact profile. Some items on The List will be negotiable. If you tick her most important boxes, she may let others slide. Maybe she wants a pianist but you play guitar. Perhaps you specialise in baklava rather than clitoris. Just as long as you are prepared to learn.

You may never discover every item on The List. And if you do, she must never know. A woman needs her mystique. You may pick up hints from time to time and maybe these can become goals - quit smoking, learn the piano, find out where the hell the clitoris is and what all the fuss is about.

You may have attributes she hadn't considered. You may be so fabulous in other ways she puts The List on hold. But, however the relationship plays out, know that The List is immortal and will one day return. Be afraid.

YOU'RE THE KIND OF

GUY

WHO KNOWS ABOUT

THE LIST

and RESPECTS IT

IT'S ONE SMALL STEP
FOR A MAN;
one GIANT LEAP
TOWARDS GETTING
SOME

SECTION TWO

SOME APPROACHES

ARISE, BRAVE SIR KNIGHT

You are exciting, perhaps even a little dangerous. Your bucket-list includes things like bungee, sky-diving, climbing Kilimanjaro, swimming with sharks and accusing heavily-tattooed, pissed footballers of being quiche-eating wankers on Mad Monday.

While actually accomplishing something is preferable, having a thrill-seeking goal or two will intrigue, maybe even tantalise her. Just the idea that you want to tackle challenging things (even the footballers) infers you are a man of action. That if she was in danger, you would be there. That you would slay a dragon for her and present her with a bracelet of its teeth.

Of course, there is a limit. The male of the species has been doing stupid shit to impress girls since the

"Hey babe, watch me ride this sabre tooth tiger!" days. Much of this has ended in disaster. Not much point telling her how much you love her while you're lying in traction and she is making eyes at the orthopaedic surgeon who can still take her dancing and has a better job than you. Whether Neil Armstrong went to the moon just to impress a chick isn't important. But it's unlikely many girls thought he was a wuss.

You should want to "suck out all the marrow of life" as poet Henry David Thoreau put it. A valiant attitude is attractive, even as mere potential. Get out there and suck some marrow. "So I went skydiving last week..." is a better conversation starter than "Check out my Xbox callouses..."

Lesser guys are too scared to pick up the phone and talk to girls. You are so far past these pitiful weaklings you can't even see them through the telescope you picked up while hiking the Andes. You aren't scared of anything - not sharks, not skydiving, not dragons, not footballers. Not even girls.

YOU ARE THE KIND OF GUY WHO HAS AN EXCITING, DANGEROUS SIDE

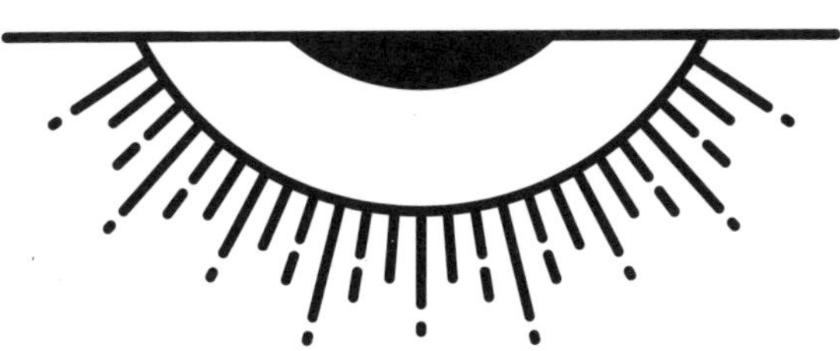

DON'T BE AN ARSE SWIPE

It's easy to churn and burn in the age of dating websites and hook-up apps. As a means to an end – meeting an actual woman – they can be very useful. Pre-qualifying a potential partner makes sense and saves time. But sooner or later you have to stop swiping in the virtual world and start living in the real one. You could spend your life swiping and one day find yourself searching www.lonesomewrinklies.com for a like-minded octogenarian with commitment issues, own teeth preferred.

Popular hook-up app Tinder is a mile wide and an inch deep. And it's largely a sausage-fest for the unfaithful. According to *The New York Times*, 30% of Tinder users are married and 62% are male. And men swipe 'like' 46% of the time while women swipe 'like' only 14% of the time. So the odds are firmly with the girls. But so are the risks.

Write your own profile – don't copy n paste another dude's or use one of the thousands of "guaranteed" pick-up lines you'll find online. Be original. Be you. Start with something fun or unusual to get her attention. 'I'm special and unique – just like everyone else.' or 'When I buy an island I'll name a mountain after you'. Anything is better than 'I like holding hands on the beach, horse riding and sunset picnics', even if you do like these things, which, let's be honest, you don't. Use current and real photos. And don't start your matched Tinder conversation with a sexual innuendo or pun.

Girls are rightly wary of hook-ups arranged online. Stick to public places, suggest she call a friend to let her know where she is and who she's with. Tell her you understand. And don't line up a series of back-to-back dates, especially at the same venue. Telling a girl her time has expired is fucked up. Build trust, not statistics.

Some dating sites do the swiping for you and recommend likely matches. Relying on a mathematical algorithm to find you a mate is the modern equivalent of an arranged marriage. You wouldn't trust your mother to hook you up so why put your faith in a series of digital optimisers that have never been kissed? Or held hands? Or brushed away a wisp of golden hair and nuzzled a sweetly scented neck? WTF would they know? Half of them are zeros anyway.

It can be tempting to stay virtual. It's like an online game. And just like gaming, it's fun, addictive and essentially pointless. For some blokes, dating apps even become their de-facto GF. Someone they turn to when they're lonely, disappointed or horny. *'Love me Tinder, Love me true…'*

Serial swipers are emotionally shallow. Smart women can spot this, especially if you are actually still swiping on a date. Serial swiping is symptomatic of a weak mind and a short attention span. Intimacy is more than a 'like'. Benching a girl as a Saturday night 'maybe' is also piss weak. If you keep churning, you'll never get far enough into a relationship to experience the joy of make-up sex.

If you sleep together after an online hook-up, call her the next day. You may have met on the internet but she is a person, not an e-conquest.

YOU'RE THE KIND OF

GUY

WHO SWIPES

for a REASON

THE HERD MENTALITY

Girls like to move in packs and cutting one out from the herd is one of the toughest challenges in courtship. You could wait for her to go to the bar or the bathroom on her own but members of the herd will often stick together for these tasks. (Why chicks go to the bathroom together is a mystery. Most blokes would rather jump in the bath with their grandmother than go to the loo with a mate.)

Approaching an assembled herd is a high-risk/high-reward strategy. Often there will be an alpha female who takes the lead in these situations. She probably has the Spice Girls line *'if you wanna be my lover, you gotta get with my friends'* as her ring tone, is protective of her herd and could be a hard-ass. You are a potential threat to her 'sisters-before-misters' ethos.

Address the herd as a group. Be polite and confident. "Good evening, girls. Are you having a good night?" Make eye contact with the object of your desires and the rest of pack at about a 50:50 ratio. She - and they -

will soon get the message. Plus, because you had the stones to tackle the herd, you have already ticked the 'courageous' box.

The herd will often giggle as a group too. Don't immediately assume they are laughing at you and run to the toilet to cry. They could be laughing at you but they may just be having a private joke and you should hang around to find out which it is. Test the water with something self-deprecating. "Normally girls don't laugh at me until I ask them out."

When the moment is right, you can make your move. "Do you mind if I borrow your friend for a minute? I promise I'll bring her right back."

Once you have her on her own, try to position her so she cannot see the herd. You have earned the right to a couple of minutes of her undivided attention. "I'm sorry to bother you. I don't want to intrude on your night out with the girls but I may never get another chance to meet you."

YOU'RE THE KIND OF GUY WHO RESPECTS THE HERD *but has* THE GUTS TO APPROACH IT

THE COMPLIMENT CONUNDRUM

Nothing will cause you to crash and burn faster than a phoney, sleazy or transparent compliment. And nothing will advance your cause more than a sincere, clever one.

"Nice tits!" may be an honest assessment but is probably best saved for post-coital cuddling.

A sincere compliment is a good way to cut the tension. Make it specific and follow up with a question: "Are you using a push-up bra or do they stand there on their own?" - if you've decided to pursue the "Nice tits" theme.

Try to avoid a compliment as your opening line. Introduce yourself first. She wants to be admired by someone she is already interested in rather than some clumsy, obvious plonker. And don't get into negging – it's stupid and disrespectful.

Compliments should be a sweet step in the dance

YOU'RE THE KIND OF

GUY

WHO MAKES OTHERS FEEL

GOOD

about

THEMSELVES

of seduction. Find something that genuinely appeals to you and go for it. Hair, clothes and eyes are safe topics. 'Lovely' and 'pretty' are better adjectives than 'hot' or 'rootable' at this early stage.

Keep it simple. "Your hair looks amazing" or "You look great in that dress" are solid compliments. Don't go in too heavy too early. "Your eyes are like limpid pools of poetic sensuality" is as inappropriate as it is nonsensical.

It is better to pass a compliment about her hair than her shoes, mainly due to the care factor. For most blokes it's difficult to care about shoes and almost impossible to compliment them without seeming gay, which is, of course, a totally acceptable lifestyle, but is, in your case, contradictory to the goal of getting some, so they (the shoes) are best left alone. If you have a fetish for towering pink stilettos with elegantly embroidered rhinestones and lace ankle straps, keep it to yourself for now.

Women wear fabulous shoes to impress other women and get great hair to impress men. They spend a fortune maintaining these two opposite ends of themselves, which is ironic as you are more interested in the bits in between.

HUMOURING HER

One of the sexiest women of her time (yes, they had sexy back in the 1950s and '60s), Marilyn Monroe advised "If you can make a woman laugh, you can make her do anything."

Girls love a man who can make them laugh. It is better if she giggles at your whimsical banter rather than your haircut, but laughter is an excellent ice-breaker and can be a powerful aphrodisiac. Funny equals quick-witted, creative and entertaining.

In comedy, as in courtship, timing is everything. You need to build trust with any audience, especially an audience you want to sleep with. The goal is to make her laugh, or at least smile. Be playful, tease nicely, avoid fart jokes. And nothing nasty or sarcastic or religious or racist or sexist, obviously. Comedy bits that killed at the pub with the boys may not transfer well to a first date. You don't want her to think your bodily functions routine is your 'A' material. Self-deprecation and faux-foolishness are winning genres. Use body language, facial expressions and change the tone of your voice. Have a (hopefully amusing) response ready to go if you crash. "Tough crowd tonight" or "Try the veal, it's as bad as me."

The principles are the same when you are texting but this is a more difficult medium because nuance and irony are less obvious, so be careful and proof read before hitting 'send'. Emoticons can help – a wink or a smiley face to show you are kidding. Have a picture of cute kittens playing in a shoe ready to send in case of emergency.

Find out what makes her laugh. Ask her about her favourite funny movies and TV shows and hope (a) you have heard of it; (b) it's not a lame rom-com; and (c) you can quote from it.

Making her laugh will relax her and possibly open her up to other types of amusement.

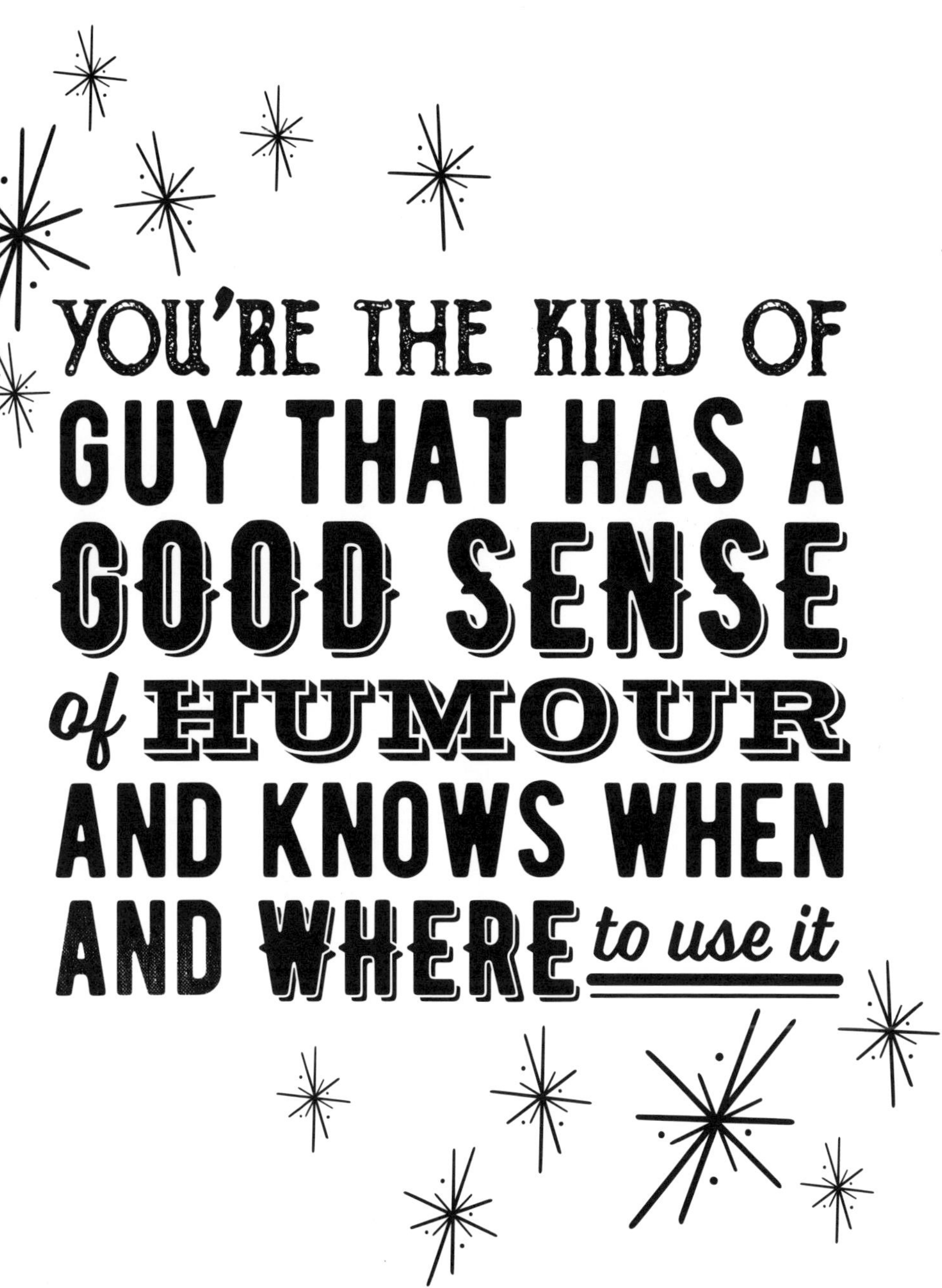
YOU'RE THE KIND OF
GUY THAT HAS A
GOOD SENSE
of HUMOUR
AND KNOWS WHEN
AND WHERE to use it

RESPECT THE EFFORT

Girls put in a humungous effort to look good for a date. They shave and pluck and wax and laser and paint and cut and primp and blow dry and do stuff that makes the boys from *Jackass* look like pussies.

It's hard work but they make it look easy and rarely complain about it. To put it in perspective, you probably had a quick shower and tried to find matching socks. And maybe clean undies, if she's special.

Already - sometimes even before you've met - you are behind. You owe her for this effort. And you will owe a little more every time you go out.

YOU'RE THE KIND OF

GUY

WHO UNDERSTANDS

AND APPRECIATES

the EFFORT

SHE MAKES

to look

BEAUTIFUL

Your acknowledgement should be in proportion to the effort she has gone to. The entry-point recognition – say, jeans and a tee shirt to go for ice cream - is that she looks amazing. An extra-special effort for a big night out requires a long, slow, wide-eyed admiration and a gushing analysis of each of the component parts from hair to shoes, followed by a summary of the whole effect. Yes, really.

She feels special when dressed to impress and she has gone to this much trouble – at least partly - for you. Tell her you are thrilled to have her on your arm. And keep the compliments coming throughout the night. Say 'Wow' a lot. And make an effort to look good yourself – make her just as thrilled to be with you. At least iron your bloody shirt.

PLAY STRAIGHT ON THE FIRST DATE

The first date should be as non-threatening as possible. Meet for a coffee or a drink rather than dinner. Never a movie – you can't talk to each other, there will likely be a leading man who is better looking than you and she shouldn't have to watch you pick popcorn out of your teeth and spill your choc-top this early in the relationship.

You probably can't win on the first date but you can certainly lose. Put getting some out of your mind. The only goal is to have fun, get to know her and land a second date.

Be well-presented and on time. Be cool if she is late, especially if you are meeting her somewhere. Girls should not have to sit alone and wait. Don't bring flowers. You can always send some ahead of the second date, if you get that far. She is probably just as nervous as you, so chill and try to make her feel comfortable. If you're having a drink together, drink at her pace.

Think of the first date as walking out to bat in a cricket match. Set yourself for a long stay at the crease. Respect the bowling and play each delivery on its merits. There is a long way to go before you raise your bat in triumph and a momentary lapse can see you dismissed without scoring. Avoid ball tampering.

Talk more about her than yourself and show interest in what she has to say. Keep it light and breezy. You can always outline your plans for a big family, your sexual predilections or your Marxist political manifesto on later dates. If she asks you what you want in a woman, do not say "my penis".

Pay for the drinks. Yes, ALL of them. If she insists on contributing tell her she can pay next time. Make sure you see her safely back to her car, home or wherever she wants to go and thank her for a lovely time. Tell her you'd like to see her again and ask if she would like to have dinner with you. Call her the next day.

YOU'RE THE KIND OF
GUY
WHO IS ALL CLASS
on the FIRST DATE

While not as crucial as First Kiss, your first physical contact can be important. We're not talking here about the initial handshake upon meeting, which should be normal, firm and equal (not dominating), and should include eye contact and a smile.

First contact is the first step towards intimacy. Watch for opportunities. As the conversation bubbles along there will be moments when you connect - a shared laugh, something you agree on, even a compliment can be reinforced with a simple touch.

When you feel such a connection, briefly touch her hand or arm. Continue chatting as if nothing happened. She will admire your confidence. A subtle first contact will make subsequent contact - and closeness - more natural.

YOU ARE THE KIND OF

GUY

who can CONFIDENTLY

INITIATE

PHYSICAL CONTACT

THE FIRST SUPPER

Sharing a meal is another make-or-break event. (Yes, there *are* a lot of make-or-break events – just deal with it.) It's unlikely she will fall in love with you over a quattro formaggi pizza or a bowl of pho but if you bugger it up, you have less chance of a happy ending than a duck in Chinatown.

Poor table manners are often a deal-breaker. If you eat like a pig, she will think you probably shag like one too. You don't necessarily have to know your salad fork from your entrée fork but the basics are important – see Do's and Don'ts of Date Dining. (And BTW the general rule for cutlery is to start from the outside and work inwards. Much like sex.)

Ask her if she has a cuisine preference and hope it's not something weird you've never heard of, like Somali or Vegetarian.

If you pick the restaurant yourself, check the reviews so if it's crap you can blame TripAdvisor.

Take care when you choosing the cuisine as it is quite difficult to eat with panache. Especially Mexican food - watch yourself eat a taco in front of a mirror and you'll understand. Barbecued ribs is not recommended either – sauce covered fingers and bibs are not sexy. If you go for Asian, practice your chopsticks – it's cool to be able to deftly lift a steamed wonton on to her plate, especially if she can't.

Italian is a safe choice. Everyone loves Italian food and the language and accent are very sexy. Italy has a culture of flirting too, which should help, as long as she doesn't fall for the super-cool dude with the designer stubble who brings her delicious food and says "*ciao bella*" with an accent that could melt mozzarella. Learn how to say a few simple words, like *grazie* (thank you), *prego* (you're welcome), *molto bene* (very good) and *vado Sergio, l'ho vista prima* (bugger off Sergio, I saw her first).

Plan the evening. Make a reservation and ask for a nice table. If it's BYO, ask her ahead of time what she would like to drink and pick it up before you pick her up. And drink what she's drinking, not your own six pack of Wild Turkey.

YOU'RE THE KIND OF
GUY WHO IS A
charming,
WELL-MANNERED
DINNER
COMPANION

DO'S AND DON'TS OF DATE DINING

Do:

- Give way to her on the way to the table without passing comment on her arse, even if it is a compliment.
- Offer to take her jacket and hand it to the waiter or hang it over her seat with care.
- Make a point of turning off (or at least muting) your phone.
- Offer her the best seat – the one with the view and/or away from the walk-through areas. Don't sit before she does. Allow her to order first.
- Order a bottle of wine or a drink that she wants. If you don't know your way around a wine list, ask the waiter to recommend one.

- Relax, smile and tell her how much you've been looking forward to the night.
- Eat slowly and chew with your mouth closed.
- Go to the bathroom to check your teeth before leaving.
- Munch a mint on the way out.

Don't:

- Preload. One drink to calm your nerves is plenty. If you're drinking, don't drive.
- Order for her.
- Order garlic unless she does. Or anything too spicy if you are prone to sweating.
- Signal the waiter by screaming "Oi!" or snapping your fingers. Always respect the staff.
- Tie your napkin around your neck or use it to flick the bums of passing waitresses. Keep it on your lap and use it regularly and subtlety.
- Dominate the conversation. Or ask her a question just as she takes a bite.
- Talk with your mouth full. A gob-full of partially masticated flesh is not a gob she will want to kiss.
- Talk about how you used to bring your ex here

and how much she loved the risotto.

- Eat food from her plate unless she offers.
- Tell her to eat all her steak and vegies to keep her strength up for later.
- Be alarmed if she doesn't eat much. This is perfectly normal for some girls, especially on first dates.
- Divide the bill into his and hers. Don't even look at it. It doesn't matter what the total is - she is worth every cent. Leave a cash tip and ask the waiter to pass on your thanks to the chef.

YOU'RE THE KIND OF GUY WHO KNOWS HOW TO *give a* LADY A GOOD NIGHT OUT

SAVE THE FIRST DANCE

Many men dance like they're resisting arrest and this is not the image you want to leave her with. This is why some blokes won't dance with a girl until well into a sexual relationship. You need to know she is serious about you before you go all the way to the dance floor.

Dancing with a girl is a very serious step. Basically, men don't look good dancing unless they're professionally trained. So if you're unco or white - or both - it may be best to feign an injury until you are sure the relationship will bear the strain of her seeing you boogie.

A minimalist approach is best - a gentle hip sway, maybe a nod and swivel. But not all at once. Avoid biting your bottom lip and bouncing and jogging movements. Do not gabber, twerk, chicken, Elaine, stage dive, headbang, robot, macarena, Harlem shake, moonwalk, achy breaky heart, Bartman, Dougie, gangnam, ketchup, stanky legg or walk like an Egyptian.

One way around the humiliation is to actually learn how to do it, but this seems like a lot of effort. If you do learn to dance, make it salsa – it's very sexy and will help to overcome your Caucasian-ness, if you suffer from that unfortunate affliction. Viva!

Make sure she understands how awkward you feel. "I can't dance, I'm awful, but for you…" And then leap to your feet and lead her confidently to the dancefloor. You may as well get the easy part right. Hopefully you will earn points for trying even if you suck once you get out there.

YOU'RE THE KIND OF

GUY

WHO IS PREPARED

TO MAKE A

GOOSE

OF HIMSELF

FIRST KISS

No pressure here, but stuff this up and you're screwed. Actually you probably won't be. The first kiss is HUGE for girls and they know what they're looking for. All you have to do is create fireworks and music in a singular crescendo of unabridged passion. Simple.

If you don't know what to do, watch a movie or Google it.

First step - be kissable. Fresh breath, no food in your teeth, a twinkle in your eye. And no matter how keen you are, try not to drool.

Be aware of the signals. Have you had fun together? Has she been flirting with you? Looking at you and smiling? Touching you? Flicking her hair? Inviting you back to her place for a shag? Admittedly some

YOU ARE A GREAT KISSER

of these signals are clearer than others but you need to have your antennae – and ONLY your antennae at this stage - up.

Be confident – she probably wants to make out too. Make and maintain eye contact. Lean in a little to instigate the kiss. She may offer you her lips, cheek or a slap in the face at this point. Kiss whatever comes your way. Open your mouth just a little at first, then more and slowly introduce the tongue. Hold her gently but firmly. Don't be the first to moan. How it goes from there will depend on her.

Don't go the grope or assume the kiss is an open invitation to access all areas. Good things come to those who wait.

TURNING GETTING SOME INTO GETTING SOME MORE

SECTION THREE

SOME COURTING TIPS

LADIES FIRST

From the moment you meet - and forever more - it's *always* ladies first. It's respectful, courteous and an indication of how you will treat her in the future. It's NOT about women being the weaker sex and needing your help and it's NOT about receiving acknowledgement. You do it because you're a gentleman.

You open the door for her. You fill her glass first. You walk on the road side of the footpath. You pay. You hold the umbrella over her in the rain – her hair *must* be protected.

Be aware that sooner or later someone will criticise your 'ladies first' ethos. Some girls will see it as sexist and even offensive. They may believe – with some justification – that it undermines equality and reflects an outdated era of paternalism. Don't argue with this attitude and don't make a big thing of it. Apologise for the unintended offence. Do not wink and slap her butt and say "I thought you Sheilas liked this shit."

YOU'RE THE KIND OF

GUY

WHO PUTS

HER

needs

FIRST

Usually, your 'ladies first' gestures will be appreciated. Chivalry is not dead but it is on the endangered list. You may be accused of sexism but you will NOT be accused of blokey selfishness.

All this is important because ill-mannered men tend to be selfish lovers. Girls hate selfish lovers. It's one of the worst things you can be. Selfish lovers are doomed.

Manners matter. Etiquette isn't just some weird relic from ancient times, like when your parents were dating. It is still appreciated and because it is rarer now, you will stand out. Stand up to meet people and always shake hands. Bugger what other people think. You'll find that other men will follow your lead and stand too. But you were the first.

Etiquette is perhaps even more important in the electronic era, when texting 'Hey' or 'Wanna?' is supposed make a girl swoon. Better to compose a long, thoughtful, engaging message and text it with a flower emoticon. Make her smile. Or even do something totally outrageous and call her! Chat to her about her day and ask her out. Wild and crazy? Sure. But it just might work. And it will certainly set you apart from the pitiful – and lazy - 'booty texting' majority.

PARTYING WITH YOUR FRIENDS

Genders often divide at parties, going their separate ways to mix with their own kind. This split along party lines is perfectly reasonable as long as it is consensual.

"Hey, baby, you go in the kitchen and find someone to crap on with about girlie shit while I hang with the boys at the keg and discuss which of you girls is the most tappable" is not as likely to generate as much ardour as "I can't wait to show you off - let me introduce you around."

After a *minimum* of an hour it may be ok to briefly wander off as long as you leave her with someone she is getting on with, she has a drink and understands she can come and find you at any time. Check back regularly to make sure she is happy. Does she need a drink, some attention, a stroke of her hair? Anticipating her needs is a powerful aphrodisiac.

Talk her up to your friends. She is beautiful and fun and you love talking about her. Don't join in drinking games unless she suggests it.

YOU'RE THE KIND OF GUY WHO LOOKS *after* HER

PARTYING WITH HER FRIENDS

You are going to be checked out, analysed and judged. While your interest in your mates' girlfriends extends to whether they have sisters, *your* girlfriend's friends will examine you like you are slime in a Petri dish. This will continue until you have met everyone she knows.

Your every move and word will be scrutinised and a detailed de-briefing will be held the next day, probably in public on the 'net. "His nails were too long." "He didn't know who Mr Darcy is." "His fly was undone the whole night." "I don't think he believes in climate change!" They may even create a Facebook page or Twitter thread (#keeplookingyoucandobetter) dedicated to the study, with sponsored links to grooming and menswear sites and Wikipedia links to Jane Austen.

It doesn't matter how fabulous you are, there will be those who find fault, for no one will ever be good enough for their lovely friend. Try not to take it too seriously – if you are on the right track with this girl you will have more opportunities to win them over. If you get too hung up on what Shaz or Kaz think, you will go insane.

All you have to do is be charming, handsome, attentive, amusing and have a great butt. So relax and enjoy yourself – it'll be no worse than a colorectal examination.

YOU'RE THE KIND OF
GUY
WHO UNDERSTANDS
her friends are
IMPORTANT
to her

GETTING SOME

Whereas you can be ready faster than you can say "You awake, babe?", girls generally take a bit longer to get into the mood. Their brains don't necessarily prioritise sex above all else. Weird, huh?

As you are well aware, blood flows to areas that receive loving caresses and you may be interested to know this applies to her bits too.

Sometimes it will be fast, furious and passionate. Sometimes it will be slow, deliberate and sensual. But usually, whatever you are doing, you are probably doing it too fast. Try to control yourself. For young men, this can be difficult but you're probably ready to go again by now anyway.

If you're getting some for the first time, expect it to be a disaster. Don't be afraid to let her know you are a virgin. If it's her first time, she will be very nervous.

YOU ARE A CARING LOVER

Be gentle and caring and make sure she is comfortable with each escalation. Do not pressure her.

Use a condom – it's *your* responsibility. If she has second thoughts or tells you to stop, you must stop IMMEDIATELY. Be understanding. This may just be a pause in proceedings but if you are a dick about it, the pause will be permanent.

Making love is about exploring and experiencing each other and lingering rather than rushing to the next level. It's not a video game. Or a race. And it's certainly not Grand Theft Auto V. You do not earn a bonus for finishing quickly.

You don't have to do everything in the Kama Sutra your first time together. In fact, keep the acrobatics to a minimum. Do not flip her over like a steak you've suddenly realised is burning on one side. This will make her feel like an anonymous piece of meat in more ways than one. The first time should be respectful and - probably - missionary. You will learn from each other and grow and improve each time. It is not possible to kiss too much. And most importantly, it is more blessed to give than receive.

SHE COMES FIRST

It's 'ladies first' in the bedroom too. As previously covered, there is nothing worse than a selfish lover. You may as well take a call from your ex during foreplay. Well, impotence isn't good either and neither are long, dirty fingernails or gerbil fetishes but you can consult a GP, manicurist or psychiatrist respectively to address these.

If this is your first time together she is probably just as anxious as you. Neither of you want it to end in disaster. She's not expecting a super-stud; just a genuine, caring effort. Be attentive to her needs and you'll do fine. And don't stress - it's supposed to be fun, for fuck's sake!

Don't overreach. Leave the hanging upside-down from the light fitting in latex undies with whipped cream aerosols in both hands for another time. Just give it your best shot, so to speak, and do what you can to help her to satisfaction. If you happen to lose control and satisfy yourself prematurely, fight your natural urge to roll over, fart and fall asleep. In all things, but especially tonight, and every night, she needs to know that if it's at all possible, she comes first.

YOU'RE THE KIND OF

LOVER

WHO PUTS

HER

NEEDS FIRST

SO NOW WHAT?

You may think the main event is over but you couldn't be more wrong. No matter how pleased you are with yourself, your post-coital moments are better spent in intimate embrace and conversation than updating your Facebook status. This is not a "well, my work here is done" moment. Afterwards is an important time for her. And for you if you ever want to go there again.

Lying together in the afterglow is about closeness. Afterglow is not a dim light by which you get dressed and sneak out. You may not be staying the night but you can afford half-an-hour (at least) to build on your connection. Try it, you just might like it. Never say "I have an early start in the morning." It is bullshit and she knows it.

Spooning is nice.

Call or text her on the way home or the next day. It is totally uncool - and amateur - to wait days to call.

DO NOT:

- Do a touchdown dance
- Scream "I DA MAN!" while thumping your chest
- Ask her to make you a sandwich or fetch you a beer
- Ask her if she thinks you've ruined her for other men
- Fall asleep or leave without telling her how much you enjoyed it
- Give your mates a blow-by-blow description or make it public in any way - classy guys don't kiss and tell

YOU'RE THE KIND OF
GUY
WHO STAYS

JUST WHEN YOU THOUGHT GETTING SOME WAS EASY, THERE'S THIS...

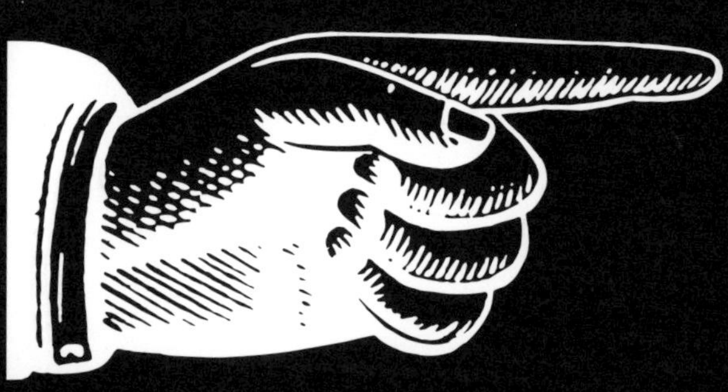

SECTION FOUR

SOME OTHER STUFF

WHAT DO WOMEN WANT?

Ah, the eternal question. And a stunningly stupid one it is too.

It is a question asked by bewildered or lazy men who don't understand people, let alone women. It's a question that tries to make his confusion her fault. It's like saying "I don't understand quantum physics, so electrons are arseholes."

The question assumes all women are the same and no one - especially women - wants the same thing all the time. The more correct question is: 'What does *your* woman want?' And yes, the answer will change regularly and you will get confused. Deal with it.

It's ok to ask her what she wants but it is better if you can figure it out yourself. Even if you have no idea, you can try to help. "Can I get you anything?" or "Would you like a shoulder rub?" are better questions than "WTF is up your arse today?"

NEVER ask her what she wants during an argument. It will always be your fault you don't know.

Allow a woman her mystery. Some questions are best left unanswered, some puzzles best left unsolved. She's like a Rubik's Cube – once you've solved it, it's not as much fun. (Spoiler Alert: Don't worry – you'll never solve it.)

YOU'RE THE KIND OF

GUY

who is NOT

THREATENED

OR ANGERED

BY A WOMAN'S

COMPLEXITY

HER BODY IMAGE

Just as you never assume a woman is pregnant unless you can actually see a baby crowning, you never suggest a change to her physique. If she asks your opinion on say, a breast augmentation, your only comment is "I love you just the way you are, but if that's what you want, of course I will support you". And don't salivate – it's unseemly.

Women are subjected to body-image stress before they can do long-division. In some cases the stress is so great they never actually learn long-division and develop an eating disorder instead. Society pressures little girls to grow up too early and then forces ridiculous ideals of perfection on them.

Most women have something they don't like about themselves. This bit is too big or too small, that bit sticks out too far, something else is too hairy or too long or too rough or too fat or too lumpy or too bony. Whether they obsess about it to the point of surgery or whether it just bothers them a little, the last thing they need is another voice in the chorus of critique. Your voice should be the one saying she is perfect now.

YOU ARE THE KIND OF

GUY

WHO SUPPORTS

and nurtures.

YOU DON'T JUST

ACCEPT HER

as she is,

YOU REVEL IN IT

TAKING A DUMP

I hold it true, whate'er befall;
I feel it when I sorrow most;
'Tis better to have loved and lost
Than never to have loved at all.

Alfred, Lord Tennyson

Tennyson's edict is probably the last thing you want to hear when you get dumped. The pain is real, the humiliation total and the torment enduring. And worse, songs by Adele and Rihanna and Tay Tay start to resonate. If it gets to this stage, seek medical attention. (Seriously though, depression can be dangerous and if you aren't functioning, talk to your GP.)

You will need time to heal and only you can decide how long. It may help to understand that as painful as it is, this is the chance for a fresh start. And your next encounter could be amazing.

How you handle a breakup counts. When the pain passes – and it will – you'll be pleased you didn't make an idiot of yourself. Grieve, sure, but don't key her car, spray paint her pets or burn angst-ridden declarations of undying devotion – or pictures of penises - into her lawn with defoliant. Singing or screaming in the rain outside her house isn't cool either. Don't call. Don't stalk. Don't be angry at other women.

The superior approach is to remain calm, unless you are being dumped for your lack of emotion, in which case you might consider the screaming in the rain option. Take it like a man. Control yourself, wish her well, kiss her on the cheek and walk away with dignity. Then you can go home, get smashed and cry yourself to sleep.

There is usually something to learn from the dump, once you get past believing the only lesson is that she's a total bitch. Did you really put all you could into the relationship? Were there warning signs you ignored? Was stealing her credit card to pay for cocaine and prostitutes really the right thing to do?

In time, you will realise that it wasn't meant to be and you will actually be relieved it ended. For if it hadn't, you would never have met the angel who is waiting for you somewhere in your future. Sooner or later nearly everyone gets their heart broken. It's part of what makes eventual true love so wonderful.

YOU ARE THE KIND OF

GUY

WHO TAKES A DUMP

QUIETLY

and with

DIGNITY

BREAKING UP IS HARD TO DO

There is no easy way to end a relationship. Breaking up should be hard. It's going to hurt her. If you find it easy to dump a girl, you're a dickhead.

Be honest but not cruel. There is no need to list her faults, even if she asks. "It's just not working for me but you're a great girl and I know you will find someone else." is better than "Seriously, I don't know what I was thinking." Or "It's not me, it's you." Or "You suck!" Or "You don't suck."

Be a man. Tell her to her face or at the very least by phone. Breaking up by text or via social media is not cool. Neither is ignoring her and doing the disappearing act known as ghosting. Or dumping her straight after sex. Or during it.

Don't cheat. You don't want to hurt someone like that. If you've met someone else, don't sleep with her until you have ended your current relationship. And don't dump her for her sister or best friend. No one deserves that.

Don't call. Especially not a booty call.

YOU'RE THE KIND OF

GUY

WHO IS AS

CLASSY

AS POSSIBLE

on either side

OF A BREAK-UP

BE A FEMINIST, MAN

"A woman without a man is like a fish without a bicycle."
- Gloria Steinem

"When a man gives his opinion, he's a man. When a woman gives her opinion, she's a bitch."
– Bette Davis

"Thou shalt not mess with women's reproductive rights."
– Fallopians 4:28

"Know what? Bitches get stuff done!"
- Tina Fey

See? Feminists can be funny. And yes, they can be other things too. Not everyone likes feminists, even some women. But the thing is, they're right. Feminism is still important. Women have been subjugated for aeons and still are to some extent, even in enlightened societies.

YOU ARE A FEMINIST

Feminists range from those seeking simple equality to feral man-haters who think women should have the right to produce their own sperm. Some believe a sexist joke is utterly abhorrent unless it's about a man. It's fun to confuse a feminist by telling her that as a man you refuse to allow her permission to get you a beer.

Real men are feminists. Real men want to end all inequality. You can open a door for a woman and still be a feminist. Whether you can open a door for a militant feminist and retain your testicles is less certain. You don't have to sing Helen Reddy's *'I am Woman'*, or Beyoncé's *'Run The World (Girls)'* at karaoke to demonstrate your cred but you should be able to sympathise with the issues. If you can't sympathise, don't say anything. Under no circumstances should you refer to feminism as 'cute'.

DEALING WITH PSYCHO LOONY MOOD SWINGS

Yeah, good luck with that.

SURVIVING PSYCHO LOONY MOOD SWINGS

ALL of us have melt-downs from time to time. Blokes like to think women have cornered the market in psycho loony behaviour but we have all been there. Most violent people and dog kickers and nasty bastards are men. So let's not get too holier-than-thou.

Women have lots of stresses and men should be aware of this. That is not to say it's ok for her to go postal on you without cause. You may get a mobile phone thrown at you for no other reason than you are in the same room but chances are you've probably done something not cool. Innocent people are sometimes found guilty, but not very often. Let he who is without sin cast the first phone.

Blow-ups in a relationship are inevitable. It's how we deal with them that counts. It is in these high-tension moments that you need to be at

YOU'RE THE KIND OF

GUY

who can

HANDLE

CONFLICT

your most understanding. Walk a mile in her ill-fitting, uncomfortable high-heels before you rush to judgement.

Some say the best way to maintain a relationship is to apologise when you are wrong and to apologise when she is wrong. This may buy you some short-term peace but it's not a viable long-term strategy. You'll end up a door mat. Remain calm and tell her you understand she is under pressure. A short-term tactical retreat is sometimes the best policy.

A little friction in a relationship can be a good thing. Show me a couple who never fight and I'll show you a couple living without passion. Again, not always, for we are not all the same. The point is conflict does not have to be a total negative. And you can't have make-up sex without a fight.

Instead of making it worse by returning fire, just listen. You might learn something. Send flowers, book her a massage or facial. Sympathise. Tell her you're there for her when she needs to vent.

SOME BASIC DO'S

- Respect her home, especially her bedroom and bathroom. Clean up after yourself.
- Lower the toilet seat. For some reason this is *huge* for chicks. If she has to put one perfect precious painted pinky on porcelain, you are worse than Hitler.
- Send gifts. Flowers are always good but putting some thought into it and sending her something that is clever, personal and creative is even better. The artist Vincent van Gogh, who cut off his ear and gave it to a girl called Rachel, is not a good role model in this regard.
- Learn to read the signals. Understanding and anticipating her needs and desires are serious turn-ons. And know that just when you have learned all the signals, they will change.
- Realise there is often a fine line between pleasure and pain. For example:
    - Confidence is sexy. Arrogance is not.
    - Modesty is sexy. Constant self-criticism is not.
    - Giving her space is sexy. Indifference is not.
    - Staying in touch is sexy. Stalking is not.

- Be assured and assuring. Be strong. Be a leader and a protector when needed, without becoming an overbearing creep.
- Ask her what she's thinking.
- Make something about her your own. (No, do not steal her underwear). Whether it be her smile, her eyes, her laugh, the curve of her shoulder, a dimple - tell her how much it appeals to you and mention it regularly.

SOME BASIC DON'TS

- Respond to a changed hairstyle with "Cool! This will be like screwing someone new!"
- Complain about having to watch a chick-flick. Bring chocolate and try to get into it. If you need to look emotional during a poignant scene, pluck a nose hair. This will produce a timely tear or two and tidy you up a bit at the same time.
- Be all about physical beauty. Whether you understand it yet or not, inner beauty is more attractive.
- Cancel a date. Unless you are in the emergency

room. Or are able to fabricate authentic sounding hospital noises over the phone.

- Talk too much about your previous relationships. Women want to know about this stuff to a point but you must make it clear it is all in the past.
- Bring baggage from old relationships into new ones.
- Be afraid to learn or adapt.
- Lose your temper or complain.
- Say you can't iron. Or cook. Or clean. Or assemble flat-pack furniture. Or buy tampons. Just bloody learn. Girls have a mothering instinct but it's not meant for you and expecting it is a serious turn-off.
- Give a shit what your mates think. Let's face it – even though you love them, your mates are idiots and it doesn't matter what they think. One man's ultra-hot mega-babe is another man's 'not even with yours, mate'. If you find her attractive, then she is and you should go for it.

For Angel

First published in 2017 by New Holland Publishers
London • Sydney • Auckland

newhollandpublishers.com

The Chandlery, 50 Westminster Bridge Road, London SE1 7QY, United Kingdom
1/66 Gibbes Street, Chatswood, NSW 2067, Australia
5/39 Woodside Ave, Northcote, Auckland 0627, New Zealand

A record of this book is held at the British Library and the National Library of Australia.

ISBN 9781742576435

Group Managing Director: Fiona Schultz
Publisher: Monique Butterworth
Designer: Catherine Meachen
Production Director: James Mills-Hicks
Printer: Hang Tai Printing Company Limited

10 9 8 7 6 5 4 3 2 1